PHONIC FOLD-UPS

Cathy Preston

World Teachers Press

Order Number 2-5045
ISBN 1-885111-59-2

C D E F   00 01

Educational Resources

395 Main Street
Rowley, MA 01969

Foreword

Phonics is seen to be an integral part of many early language programs. *Phonic Fold-Ups* is a book designed to make phonics interesting and enjoyable for children and allows the teacher an alternative strategy for the teaching, application and reviewing of phonic sounds. The book takes students through a series of two and three-letter blends, which can occur at the beginning and the end of a word. The activities are designed to introduce and reinforce particular phonic sounds.

The method of completion and construction is simple and allows the student to finish the activity with a product or evidence of their progress which can be taken home or shown to other students and develop personal pride and recognition of progress.

Index of Sounds

Teacher Information

The following is a development plan using one of the pages in this book. It is an example of how the activities in this book could be introduced, developed and extended.

Introducing Work

Introduce the children to the phonic sound 'bl' giving some examples of words which explain this sound. Encourage discussion and brainstorming in which children are required to offer other words which may have this sound.

Lesson Development

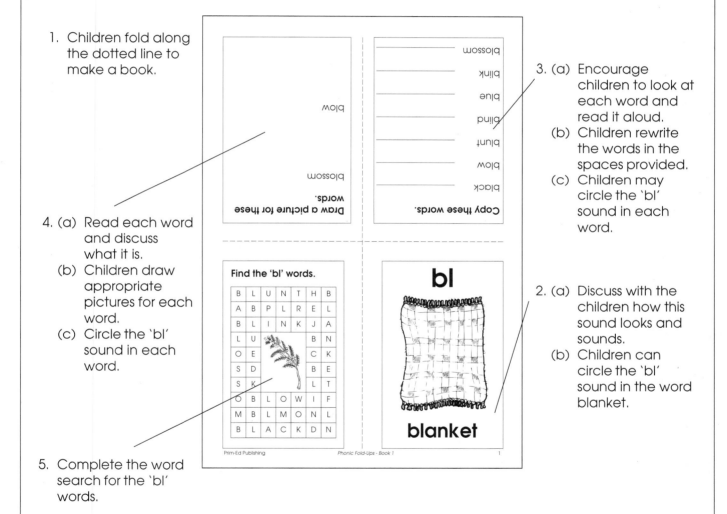

1. Children fold along the dotted line to make a book.

4. (a) Read each word and discuss what it is.
   (b) Children draw appropriate pictures for each word.
   (c) Circle the 'bl' sound in each word.

5. Complete the word search for the 'bl' words.

3. (a) Encourage children to look at each word and read it aloud.
   (b) Children rewrite the words in the spaces provided.
   (c) Children may circle the 'bl' sound in each word.

2. (a) Discuss with the children how this sound looks and sounds.
   (b) Children can circle the 'bl' sound in the word blanket.

Extension

Once children complete the phonic booklet, they may be encouraged to write sentences on their own using the 'bl' words.

The fold-a-book can also be used as a home reader to reinforce the phonic sound studied in class.

9

Draw pictures for these words.

blossom

blow

Copy these words.

black

blow

blunt

blind

blue

blink

blossom

Find the 'bl' words.

B	L	U	N	T	H	B
A	B	P	L	R	E	L
B	L	I	N	K	J	A
L	U				B	N
O	E				C	K
S	D				B	E
S	K				L	T
O	B	L	O	W	I	F
M	B	L	M	O	N	L
B	L	A	C	K	D	N

---

bl

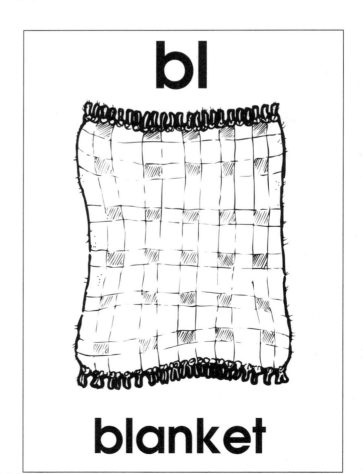

blanket

Unjumble the 'cl' words.

eevcrl

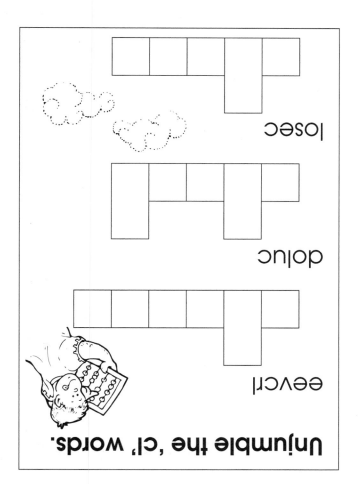

doluc

losec

Copy these words.

cloud _____

clock _____

close _____

cluck _____

clever _____

clear _____

class _____

Draw a clown with a clock in his hand.

cl

clown

Copy these words.

flock _____

flour _____

float _____

flash _____

flood _____

floor _____

flounder _____

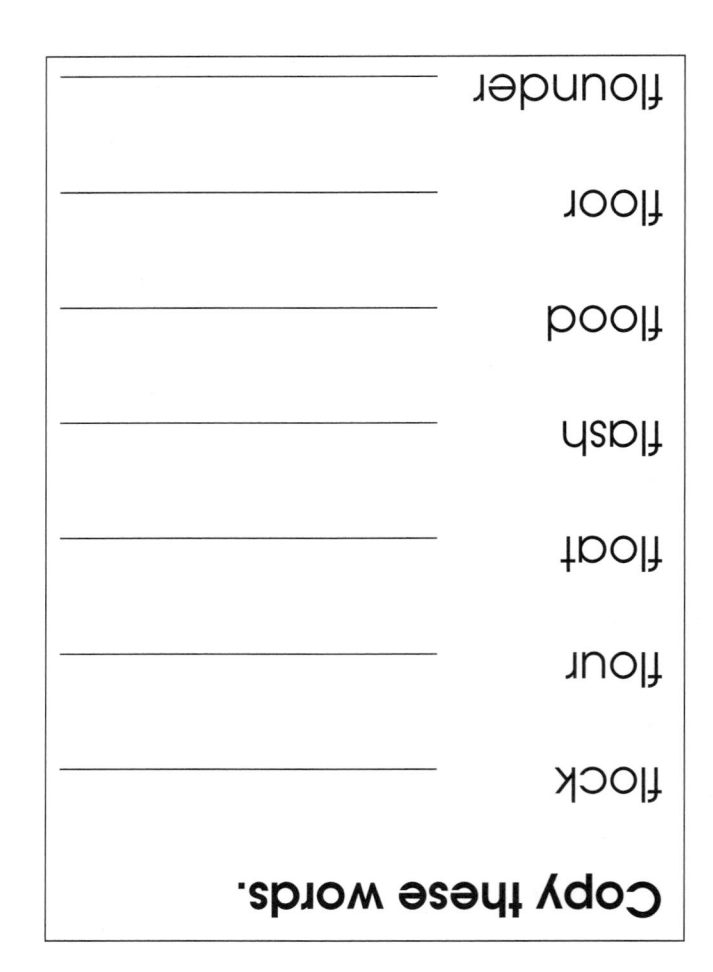

Complete these 'fl' words.

fl _ _ p

f _ _ or

fl _ _ k

fl _ _

f _ _ ur

f _ _ h

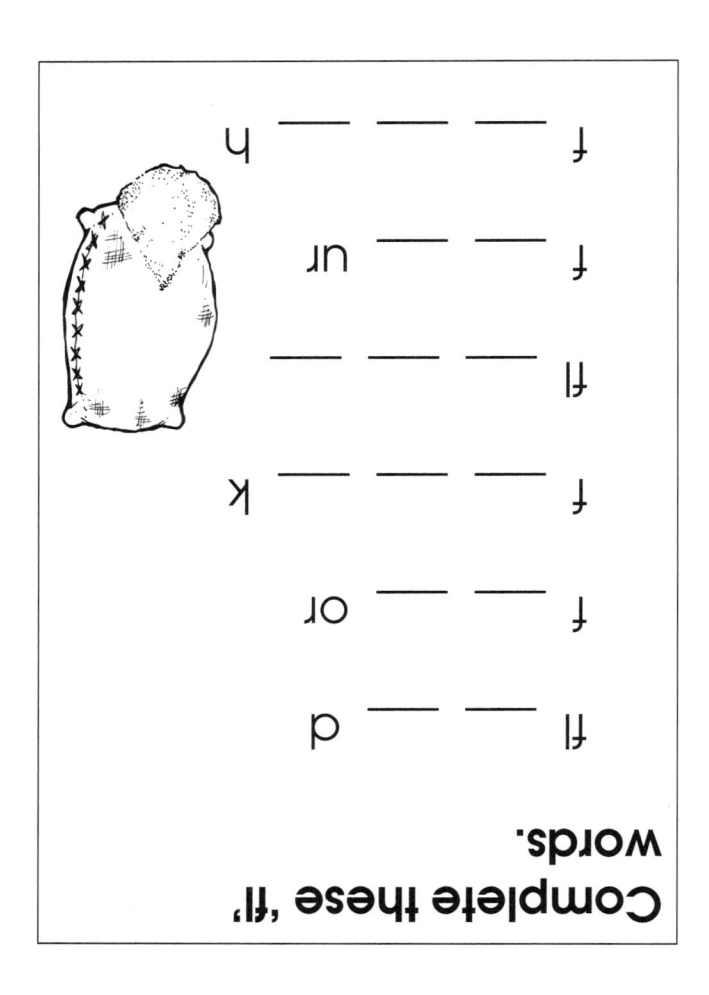

Find and color the 'fl' words.

memrtdfgeflashbnjoftrh
flounderkvtoflockc
jgtflowerhettfastfloat
fnfloorrsldlflourffloodm

fl

flower

glue

gl

Circle the 'gl' words in the sentence. Draw a picture of the sentence.

'I used a glove to pick up the hot globe.'

Copy these words.

glove _____

glare _____

glide _____

glad _____

glass _____

globe _____

gleam _____

Match the 'gl' words to their meanings.

glad • • to fly

glue • • to shine

glide • • an angry look

gleam • • happy

glare • • to stick together

Match the 'pl' words to their pictures.

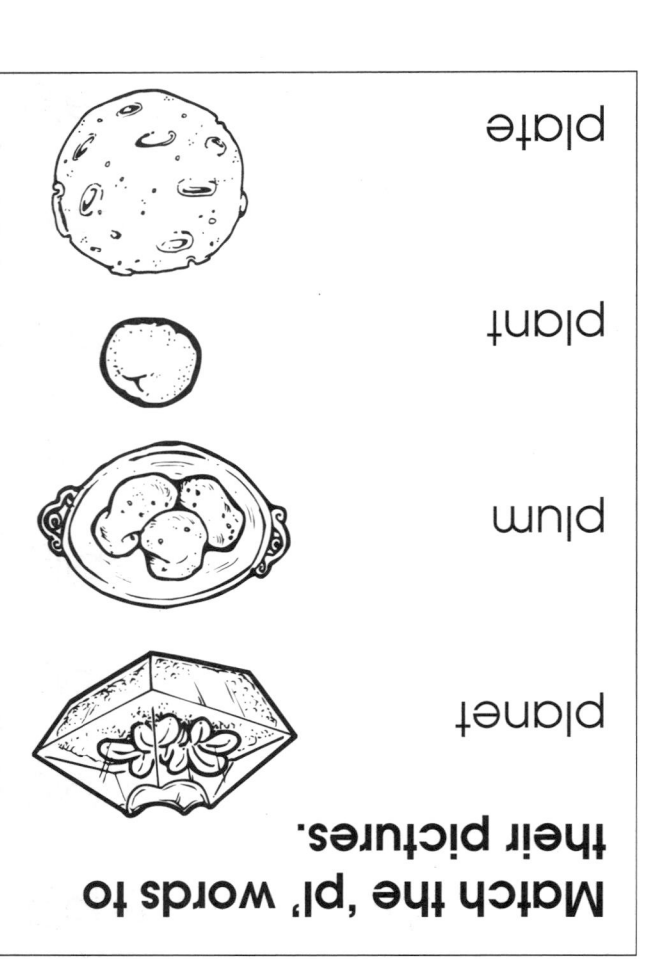

planet

plum

plant

plate

Copy these words.

planet _____

plastic _____

plenty _____

plum _____

plant _____

please _____

plate _____

Color the correct answer.

A plant is a type of rock.
Yes   No

A plum is a fruit. Yes   No

The Earth is a planet.
Yes   No

It is rude to say please.
Yes   No

A plant is a type of dog.
Yes   No

pl

playground

Copy these words.

slave

slim

sling

slam

slow

sleeve

slipper

Complete the 'sl' words.

ave   ow

ing   im    sl   ipper

---

sl

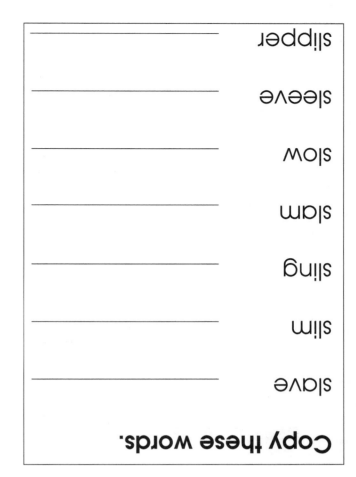

sleep

Complete the crossword.

slam
slave
slim
sleeve

i

v

e   v

Find the 'br' words.

B	R	I	G	H	T	B
R	A	R	I	J	B	R
A	B	R	U	S	H	A
N	B				B	V
C	R				R	E
H	E				O	F
R	E				W	E
C	Z	B	E	D	N	E
R	E	B	R	E	A	D
B	R	E	A	K	R	F

br

bread

Draw pictures for these words.

branch

brush

Copy these words.

brave

break

brown

brush

branch

bright

breeze

Copy these words.

crayon

crawl

crow

cream

crash

creek

creak

Unjumble these 'cr' words.

eakrc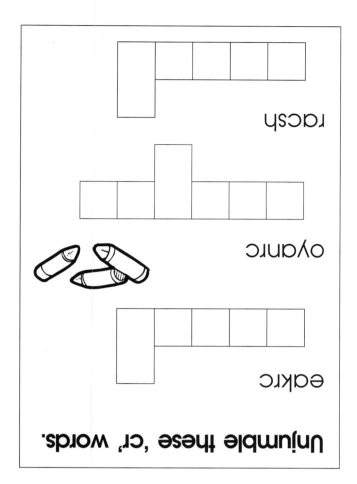

oyanrc

racsh

Draw a crow and a crab near a creek.

cr

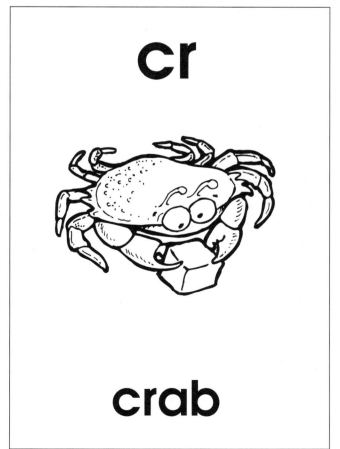

crab

Complete these 'dr' words.

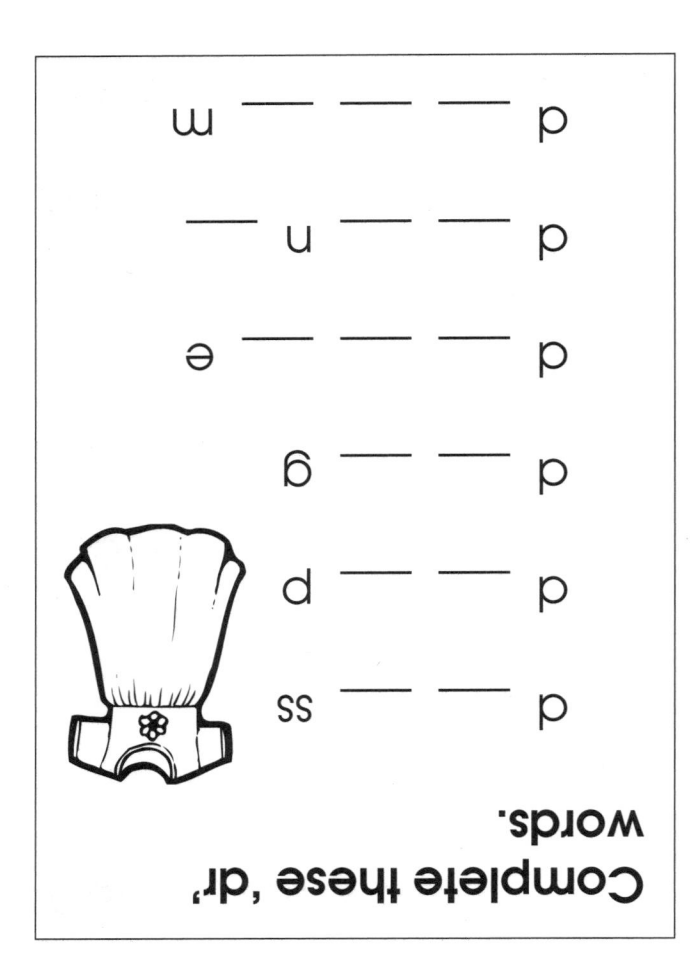

p — m
p — n
p — e
p — g
p — d
p — ss

Copy these words.

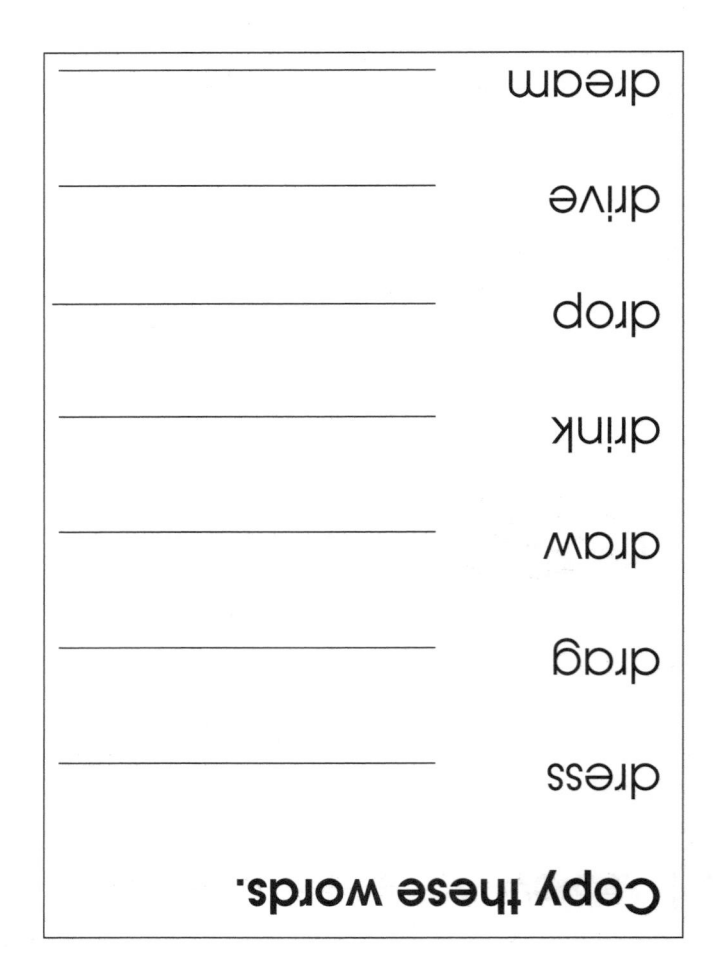

dream _____

drive _____

drop _____

drink _____

draw _____

drag _____

dress _____

Find and color the 'dr' words.

dreamabopddrink

puytdropnmwerdressmk

mwndrawasddragonbcv

tdragnhuiwdrivelo

dr

dragon

Phonic Fold-Ups

Match the 'fr' words to their meanings.

frill • • a small animal

frown • • new

fresh • • a type of food

fruit • • a worried look

frog • • a ruffled edge

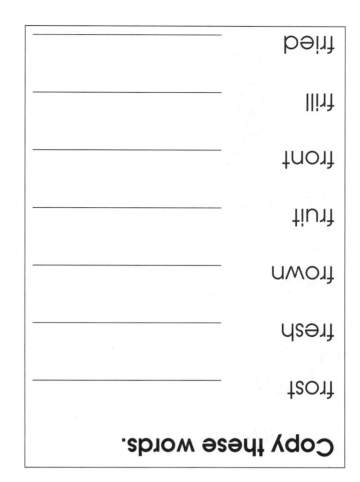

Copy these words.

frost _____

fresh _____

frown _____

fruit _____

front _____

frill _____

fried _____

Circle the 'fr' words in the sentence. Draw a picture of the sentence.

'The frog liked eating fresh fruit.'

fr

frog

Match the 'gr' words to their pictures.

growl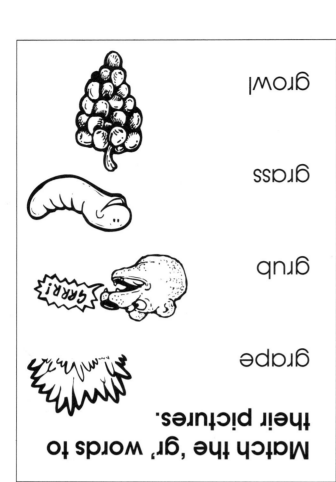

grass

grub

grape

Copy these words.

grass _____

grow _____

grab _____

ground _____

green _____

growl _____

grub _____

Color the correct answer.

A grape is a type of fruit.
Yes No

Green is a color.
Yes No

A grub is a type of tree.
Yes No

The ground can be found in the sky.
Yes No

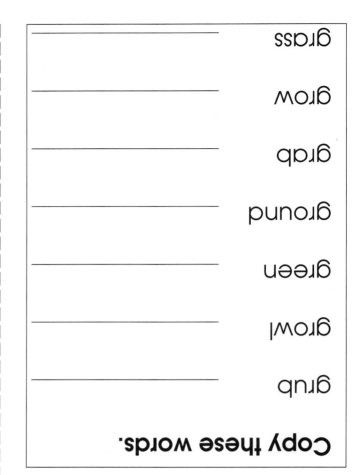

gr

grow

Phonic Fold-Ups
World Teachers Press

Complete the 'pr' words.

etty   esent

ess   am   pr   ice

Copy these words.

price

prawn

prince

print

press

prize

pretty

Complete the crossword.

prince
price
prize
pretty

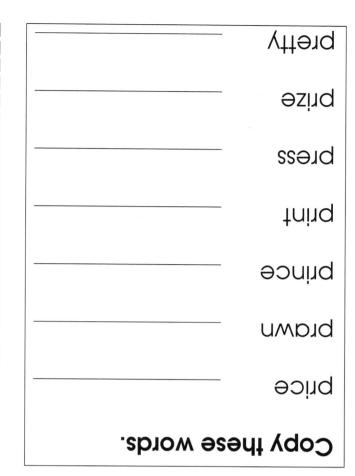

$1.00

				c	
		z			
	c				
e			y		

---

pr

prawn

Draw pictures for these words.

trumpet

tray

Copy these words.

trunk

trot

tray

truck

trick

trumpet

trouble

Find the 'tr' words.

T	R	U	C	K	L	T
A	T	I	R	E	T	R
T	R	A	I	N	H	U
K	O				D	M
Y	T				T	P
J	A				R	E
E	T				U	T
G	T	R	A	Y	N	B
C	T	R	I	C	K	F
T	R	O	U	B	L	E

tr

train

Unjumble the 'sc' words.

owlsc

hctarcs

laesc

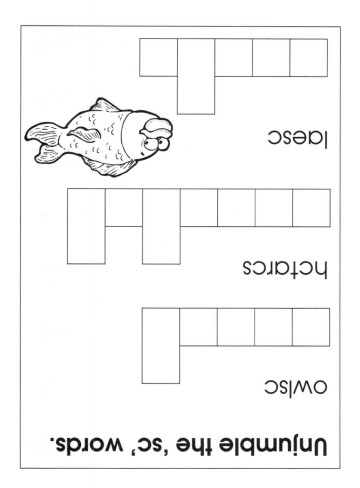

Copy these words.

scan _____

scar _____

scale _____

scare _____

score _____

scarf _____

scowl _____

Draw a scar on the scale of a fish.

---

sc

scarf

Phonic Fold-Ups World Teachers Press

Complete these 'sk' words.

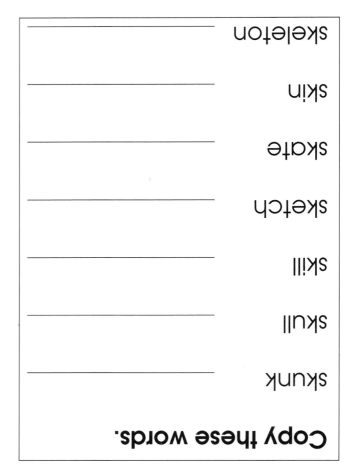

sk — —

sk — — e

sk — — h

sk — — l

sk — — k

ske — t — — n

Copy these words.

skeleton _____

skin _____

skate _____

sketch _____

skill _____

skull _____

skunk _____

Find and color the 'sk' words.

skunkmsfrskatemns
mskadreskeletonnkgskb
oskullbgtsskillbresdskipli
hstskinteousketchi

sk

skunk

Match the 'sn' words to their meanings.

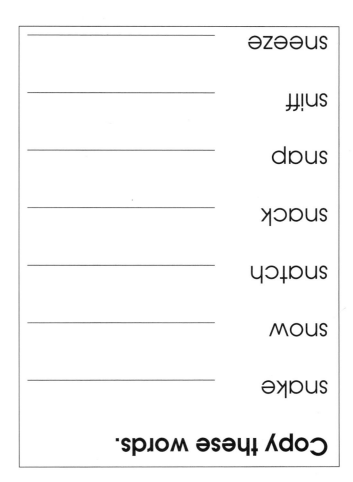

snail • • to smell

snack • • frozen water

snap • • a reptile

sniff • • to break

snow • • a small animal

snake • • a small meal

Copy these words.

sneeze _____

sniff _____

snap _____

snack _____

snatch _____

snow _____

snake _____

Circle the 'sn' words in the sentence. Draw a picture of the sentence.

'The snake and the snail are in the snow.'

sn

snow

Match the 'sm' words to their pictures.

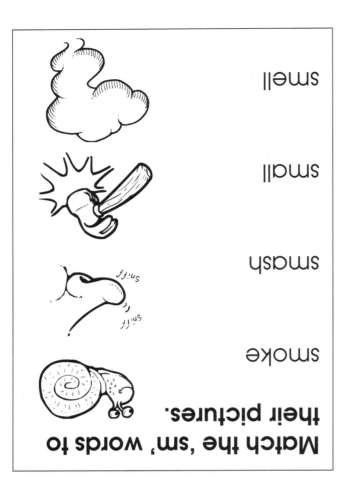

- smoke
- smash
- small
- smell

Copy these words.

- smooth _____
- small _____
- smash _____
- smack _____
- smell _____
- smart _____
- smoke _____

Color the correct answer.

An elephant is small.
Yes No

Glass is smooth. Yes No

You are sad when you smile. Yes No

Smoke comes out of chimneys. Yes No

An ant is small.
Yes No

sm

smile

Complete the 'sp' words.

sp

in   ine   ill

ade   rint

_____
_____
_____
_____
_____

Copy these words.

spin
spine
speed
special
spade
spill
sprint

_____
_____
_____
_____
_____
_____

Complete the crossword.

special
spin
spill
spine

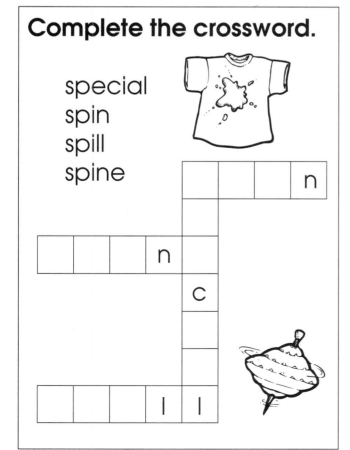

sp

sport

Copy these words.

last

fast

first

step

start

gust

stick

Draw pictures for these words.

stick

step

Find the 'st' words.

S	S	T	E	P	F	S
M	T	G	G	U	A	T
C	A	U	Y	B	S	I
S	R				T	C
T	T				S	K
S	G				E	O
A	A				T	G
L	I	S	T	A	R	U
P	R	L	S	A	D	S
F	I	R	S	T	S	T

st

start

Phonic Fold-Ups

Unjumble the 'sw' words.

wings

weeps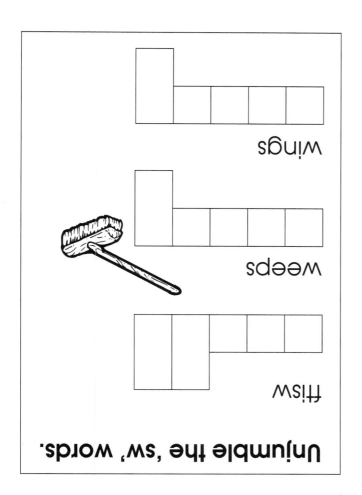

swift

Copy these words.

swamp _____

swap _____

sweet _____

sweep _____

swarm _____

swing _____

swift _____

Draw a swan flying over a swing.

SW

swan

Complete these 'lt' and 'mp' words.

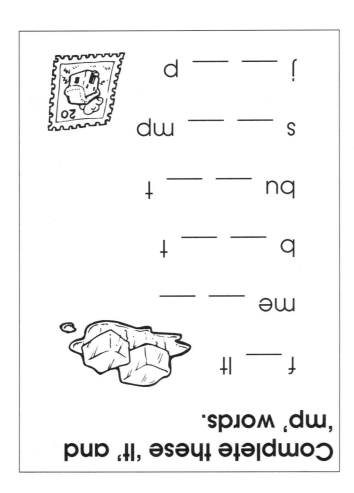

j — — p

s — — mp

bu — — t

b — — t

me — —

lt f — —

Copy these words.

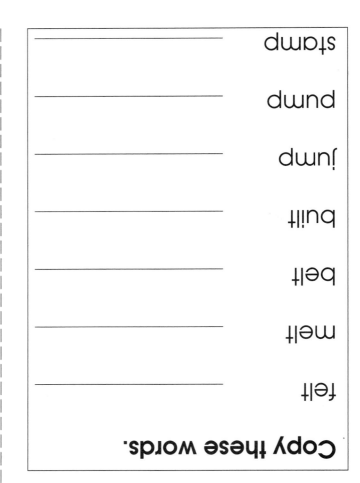

felt _____

melt _____

belt _____

built _____

jump _____

pump _____

stamp _____

Find and color the 'lt' and 'mp' words.

pumpgsrweejstampjhgs ldfepjfeltopgsmelt plsbeltksplwndbuiltmkiu ftjumpbeeklampjrq

lt

belt

mp

stamp

Phonic Fold-Ups World Teachers Press

Copy these words.

mend _____
ant _____
bend _____
friend _____
dent _____
paint _____
hand _____

Match the 'nt' and 'nd' words to their meanings.

tent •   • to fix

ant •   • a person that likes you

mend •   • part of the body

hand •   • an insect

friend •   • a shelter

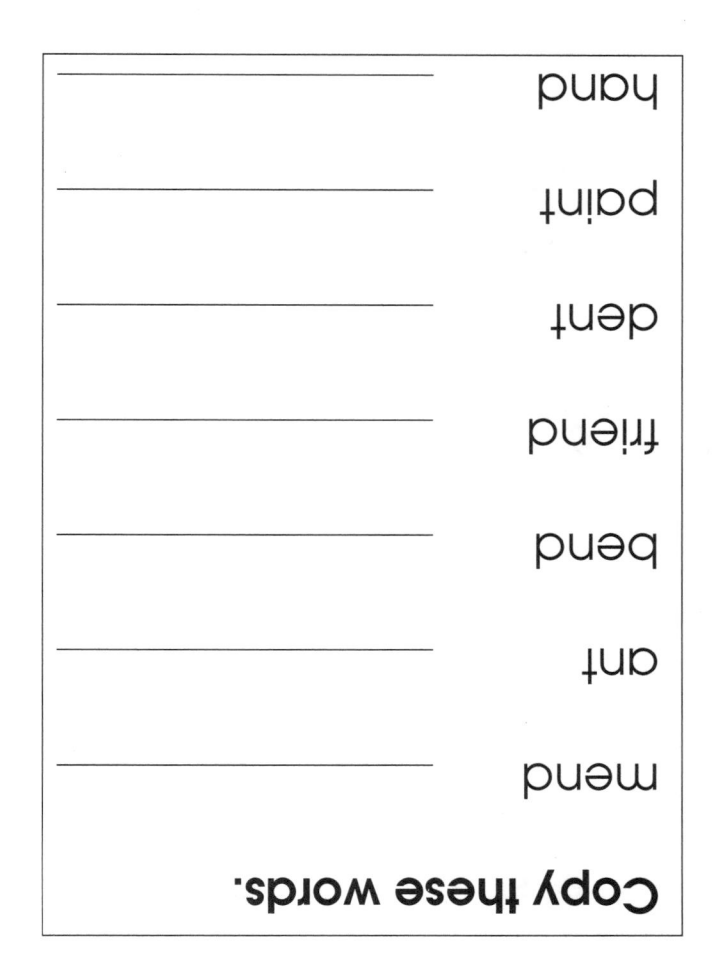

Circle the 'nt' and 'nd' words in the sentence. Draw a picture of the sentence.

'The ant was on my hand in a tent.'

nt

tent

nd

hand

Match the 'tw' words to their pictures.

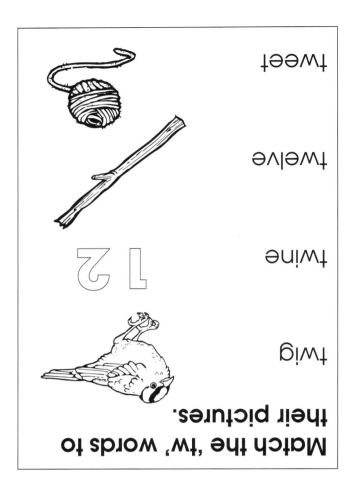

twig

twine

twelve

tweet

Copy these words.

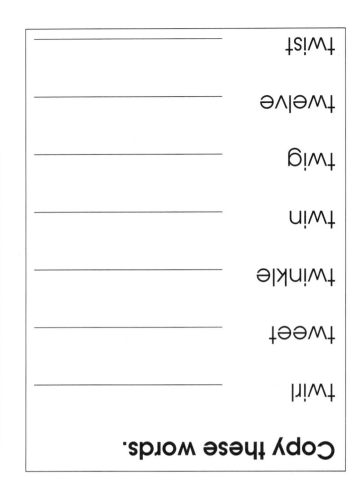

twirl _____

tweet _____

twinkle _____

twin _____

twig _____

twelve _____

twist _____

Color the correct answer.

A twin is one of two.

[Yes] [No]

Twine is a type of animal.

[Yes] [No]

Twelve is the next number after nine.

[Yes] [No]

A twig is part of a plant.

[Yes] [No]

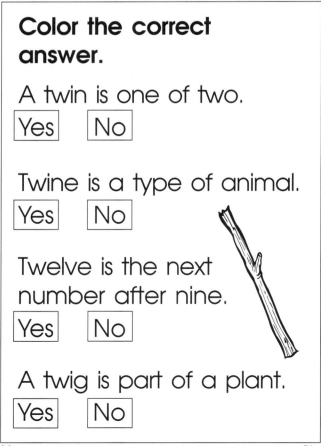

tw

twins

Copy these words.

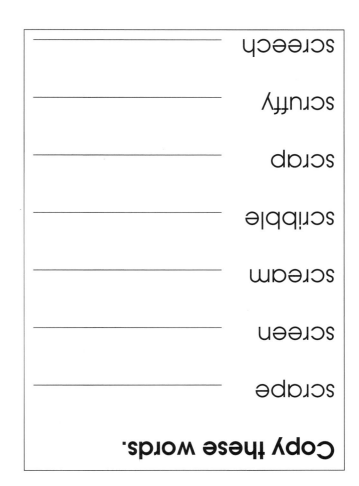

scrape

screen

scream

scribble

scrap

scruffy

screech

Complete the 'scr' words.

eam   scr   ape   ap

uffy   een

Complete the crossword.

scrap
scrape
scream
screen

p

a m

p

e e

scr

scrub

Find the 'spl' and 'spr' words.

S	P	L	A	S	H	S
P	S	G	S	A	F	P
R	P	P	Y	R	S	R
E	L				P	I
A	I				L	N
D	N				I	G
P	T				N	L
E	S	P	L	I	T	E
S	P	R	A	Y	E	C
S	I	A	H	B	R	D

spl

splinter

spr

spread

str

strong

Draw a straw with a stripe near some string.

Copy these words.

street

stream

strong

string

stripe

strange

streamer

Unjumble these 'str' words.

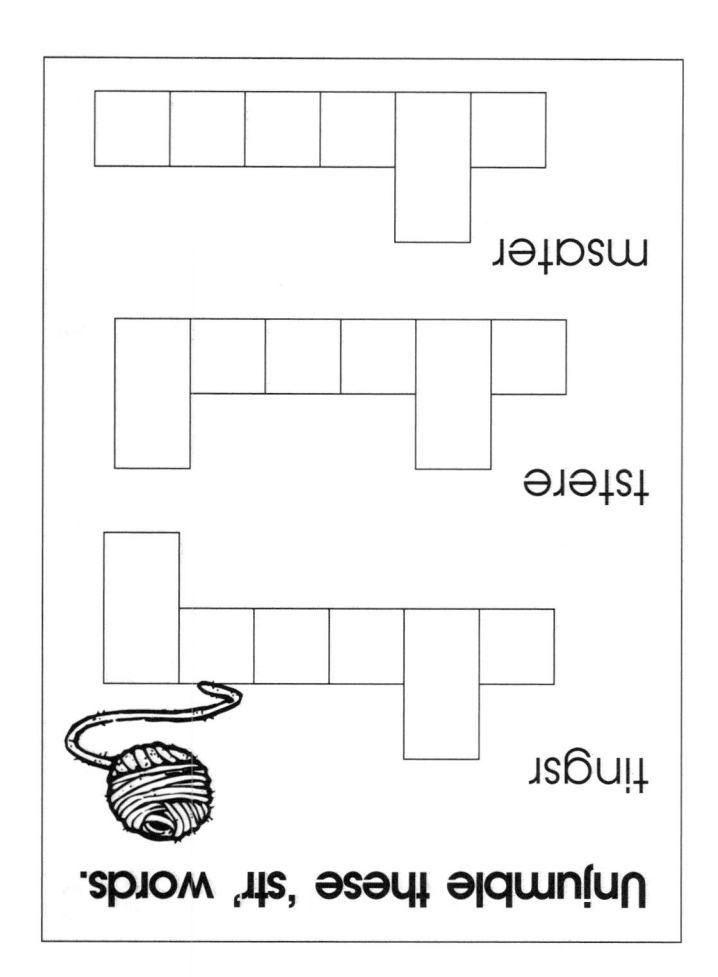

tingsr

tstere

msater

Copy these words.

rung

stung

hunger

fang

bang

rang

clang

Draw pictures for these words.

rang

bang

Find the 'ung' and 'ang' words.

R	U	N	G	A	C	B
A	G	E	U	J	L	A
N	S	A	N	G	A	N
G	B				N	G
G	D				G	H
I	R				A	F
N	N				M	A
S	T	U	N	G	B	N
C	K	N	F	L	S	G
H	U	N	G	E	R	G

ung

stung

ang

clang

Phonic Fold-Ups World Teachers Press

Unjumble the 'ing' words.

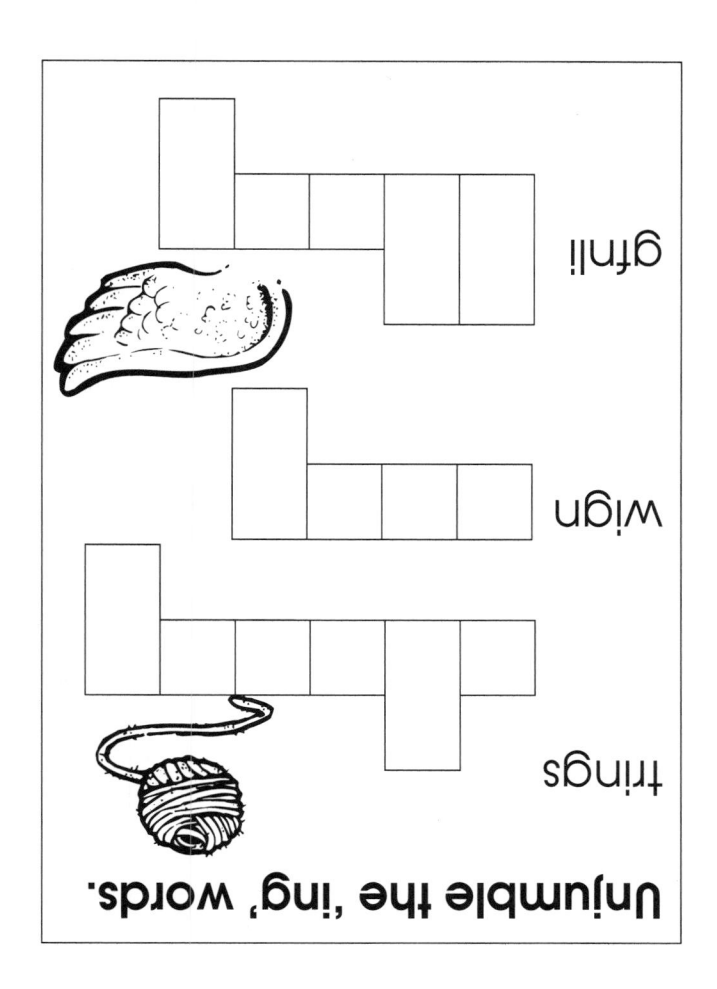

gfnil

wign

trings

Copy these words.

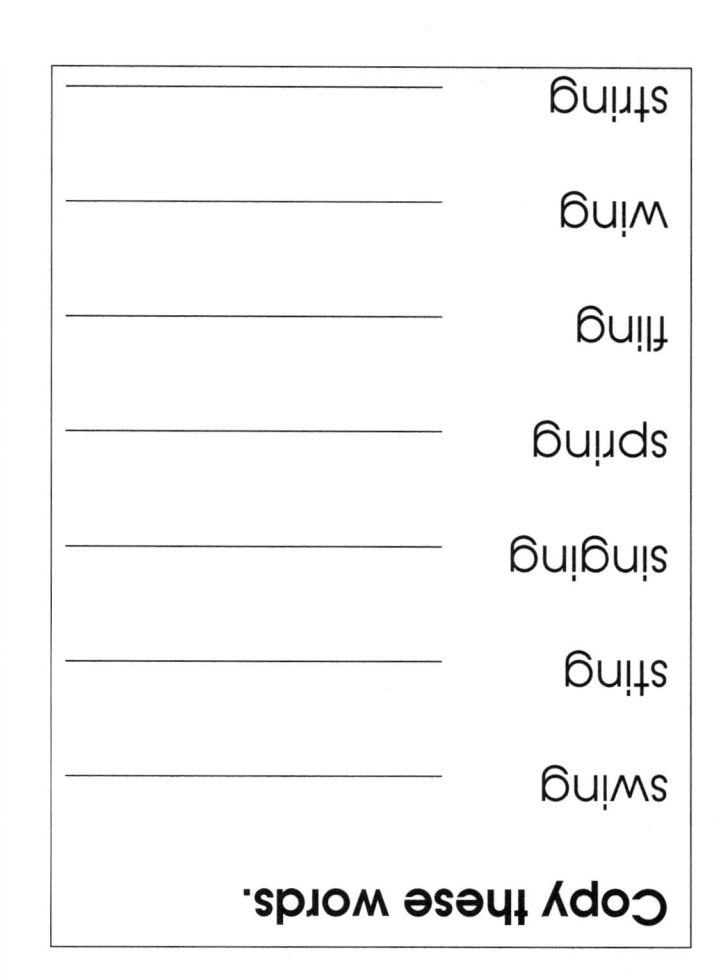

string

wing

fling

spring

singing

sting

swing

Draw a boy on a swing in spring.

ing

ring

Complete these 'ank' words.

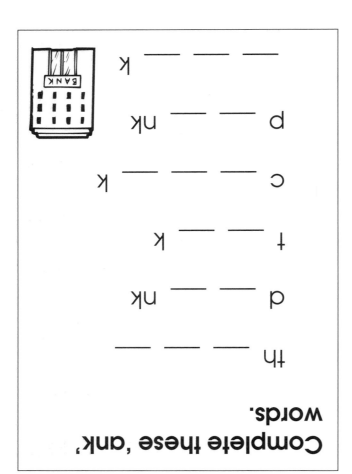

- th _ _ _
- p _ _ nk
- t _ _ k
- c _ _ k
- p _ _ nk
- _ _ _ k

Copy these words.

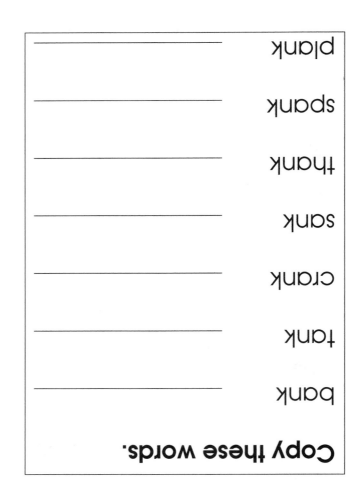

bank _____

tank _____

crank _____

sank _____

thank _____

spank _____

plank _____

Find and color the 'ank' words.

banklmandtankmm
hbrtsdsankmtsbplanktw
ertcrankoptyspank
wpothanklopkndranklw

ank

drank

34   *Phonic Fold-Ups*   World Teachers Press

Match the 'ink' words to their meanings.

pink • • a basin with water

shrink • • a color

drink • • to make smaller

sink • • to swallow

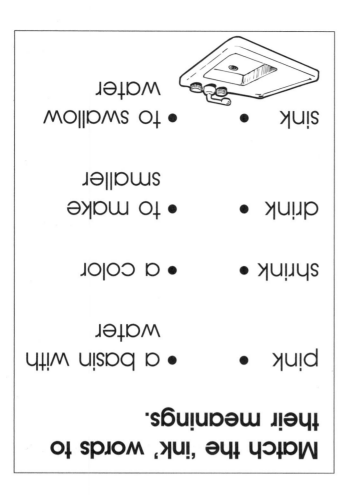

Copy these words.

pink _____

think _____

sink _____

twinkle _____

shrink _____

blink _____

rink _____

Circle the 'ink' words in the sentence. Draw a picture of the sentence.

'The girl with the pink dress was having a drink'

ink

think

Match the 'ill' and 'ell' words to their pictures.

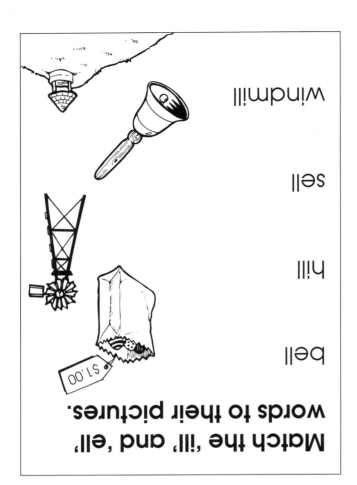

bell

hill

sell

windmill

Copy these words.

sell _____

fell _____

bell _____

windmill _____

fill _____

hill _____

still _____

Color the correct answer.

A shell is a type of road.

Yes   No

A bell makes sound.

Yes   No

To sell is to buy something.

Yes   No

Fill is opposite to empty.

Yes   No

ill

hill

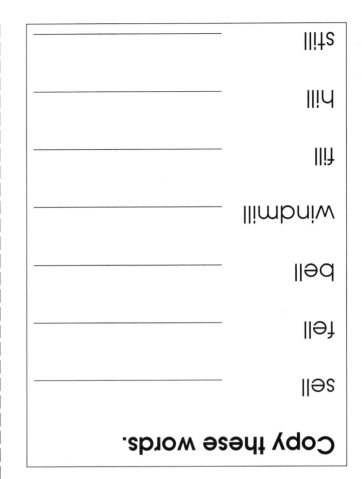

ell

shell

Phonic Fold-Ups

Complete the 'ull' and 'oll' words.

g ull sk

d oll j - y h - y

Copy these words.

gull

skull

dull

roll

gully

jolly

holly

Complete the crossword.

gully
pull
full
doll

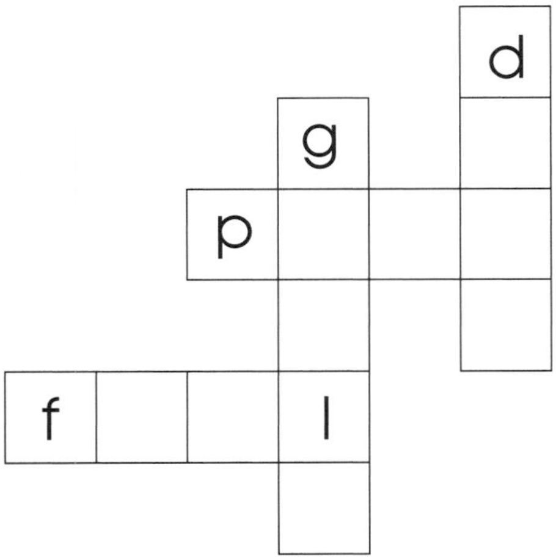

ull

gull

oll

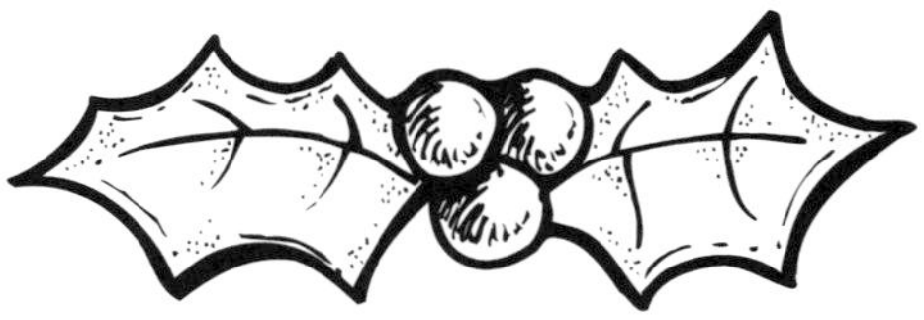

holly

Draw pictures for these words.

cold

old

Copy these words.

bold

old

fold

hold

cold

gold

fold

Find the 'old' words.

S	O	K	A	O	L	D
O	A	B	H	P	G	L
L	M	C	O	L	T	O
D	D				G	C
O	L				G	F
A	O				O	O
A	H				L	B
I	D	L	O	F	D	O
K	J	B	C	D	O	L
T	O	L	D	E	L	D

old

gold

Phonic Fold-Ups

squid

squ

Draw a squid with a
squirrel.

Copy these words.

squirt _____

squint _____

squirrel _____

squeal _____

squeeze _____

squash _____

squelch _____

Unjumble the 'squ' words.

trisuq

lrisqure

tinusq

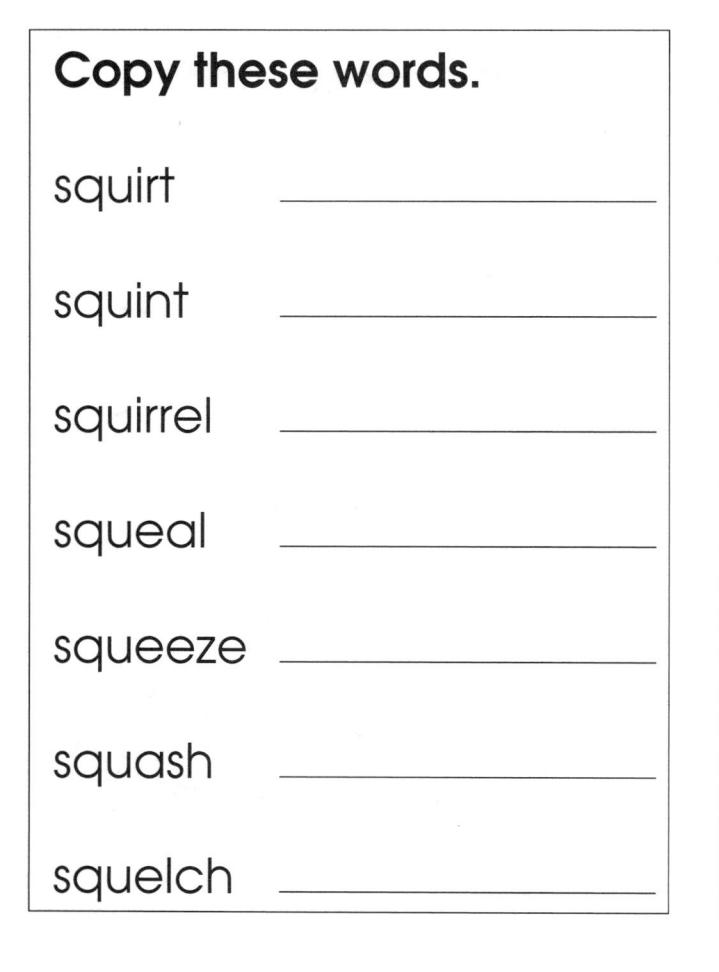

Complete these 'ch' words.

ch _ _ _ se

ch _ in

_ _ _ r

ch _ _ d

_ _ _ est

c _ _ p

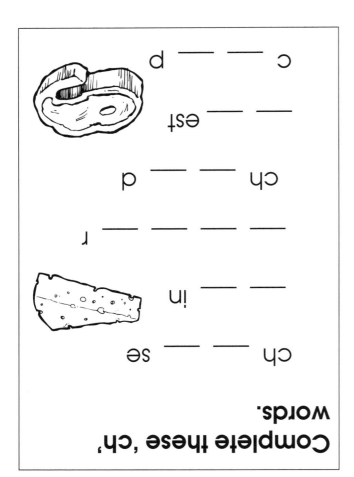

Copy these words.

cheese _____

chop _____

chest _____

child _____

rich _____

cheer _____

chin _____

ch

chicks

Find and color the 'ch' words.

chinmmfgdrichmsd
cheese   rwchildmnchjilichopmns
mnvchscchestbn   chichickmdcheert

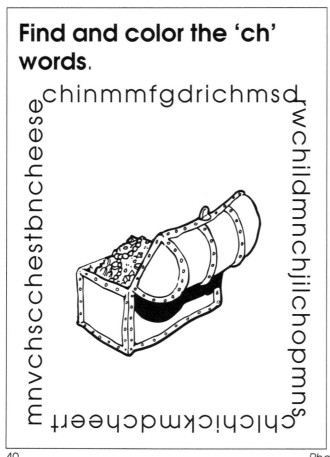

Copy these words.

finish _____

shoe _____

fish _____

shop _____

wish _____

shut _____

brush _____

Match the 'sh' words to their meanings.

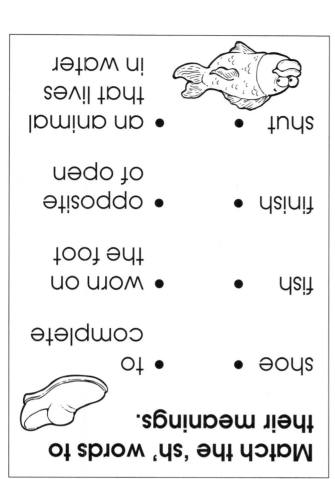

shoe • • to complete

fish • • worn on the foot

finish • • opposite of open

shut • • an animal that lives in water

---

sh

ship

Circle the 'sh' words in the sentence. Draw a picture of the sentence.

'The fish bought a brush from the shop.'

Match the 'th' words to their pictures.

thumb

thunder

moth

thin

Copy these words.

thin _____

thick _____

thank _____

thumb _____

thud _____

thunder _____

moth _____

Color the correct answer.

Thick is the same as thin.

Yes   No

A moth is a type of bird.

Yes   No

A 'thud' is a type of sound.

Yes   No

Thunder can happen in storms.

Yes   No

th

thief

Phonic Fold-Ups

Copy these words.

whip

where

wheel

whisper

white

wheat

why

Complete the 'wh' words.

ere   ite

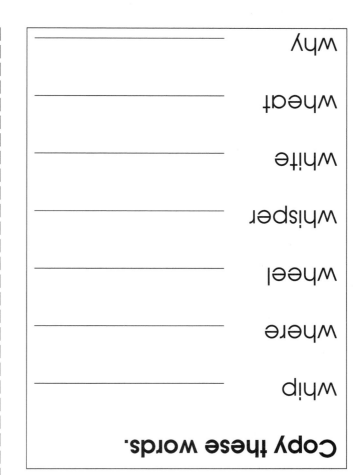

wh

eel   isper   ale

Complete the crossword.

where
whale
whisper
wheel
whip

	h		l	e
				l
	p			
		r		

wh

whale

Draw pictures for these words.

trick

sock

Copy these words.

black _____

sock _____

clock _____

rock _____

trick _____

block _____

sick _____

Find the 'ck' words.

D	U	C	K	A	K	B
T	N	S	O	C	K	L
R	E	M	G	B	C	A
I	O				B	C
C	C				L	K
K	D				O	C
J	I				C	L
F	K	K	T	C	K	O
S	I	C	K	L	K	C
L	E	W	R	O	C	K

ck

duck

Unjumble these 'nch' words.

cenbh

canrh

huncp

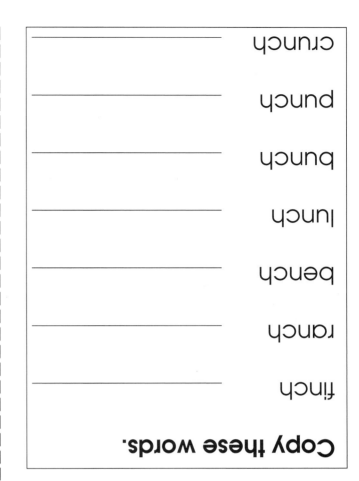

Copy these words.

finch

ranch

bench

lunch

bunch

punch

crunch

Draw a finch on a branch.

nch

branch

tch

witch

Copy these words.

hutch _____

catch _____

match _____

stitch _____

switch _____

itch _____

scratch _____

Complete these 'tch' words.

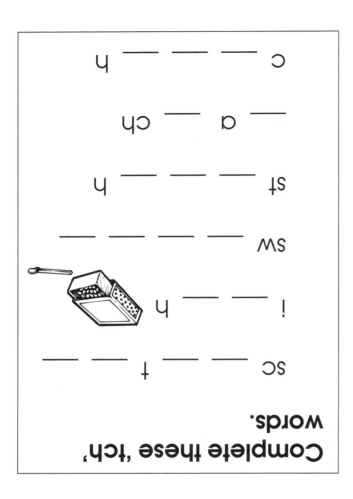

sc _ _ t _

_ _ _ _ h   i

sw _ _ _ _

st _ _ _ h

_ a _ _ ch

c _ _ _ h

Find and color the 'tch' words.

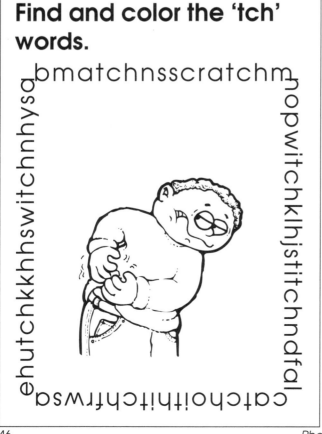

bmatchnsscratchm
ehutchkkhhswitchnhysa
nopwitchklhjstitchnddfal
catchoithitchftwsa

Copy these words.

thrill

three

thrush

throat

thrash

throw

through

Match the 'thr' words to their meanings.

- throw • • the chair of a king or queen
- thrash • • to fling into the air
- throne • • a number
- three • • a part of the body
- throat • • to beat

Circle the 'thr' words in the sentence. Draw a picture of the sentence.

'The three children had to throw the balls through the hoop."

---

thr

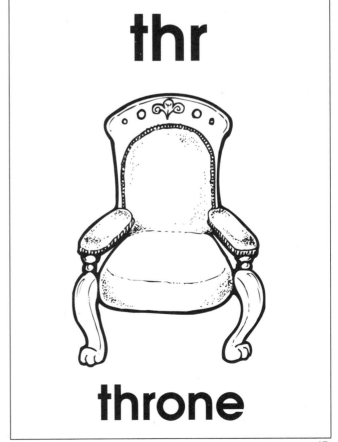

throne

Match the 'ar' words to their pictures.

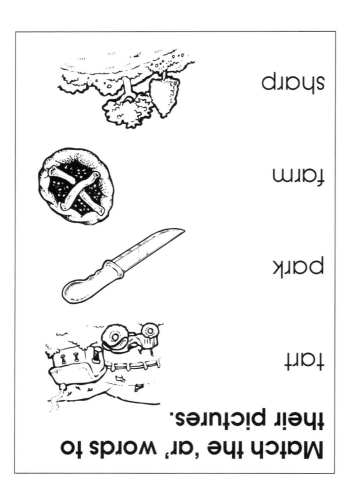

sharp

farm

park

tart

Copy these words.

start _____

mark _____

park _____

farm _____

sharp _____

tart _____

march _____

Color the correct answer.

A shark lives in the water.
Yes   No

A tart is a type of plant.
Yes   No

Start is the opposite of finish.
Yes   No

A march is a type of horse.
Yes   No

ar

shark

48   *Phonic Fold-Ups*   World Teachers Press

Complete the 'er' words.

riv   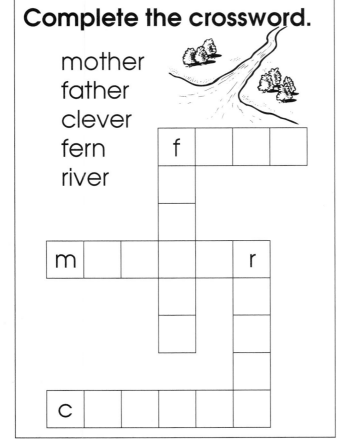 er   ladd

clev   jump   moth

_____

_____

_____

_____

_____

Copy these words.

river

fern

clever

gather

mother

father

jumper

_____

_____

_____

_____

_____

_____

_____

Complete the crossword.

mother
father
clever
fern
river

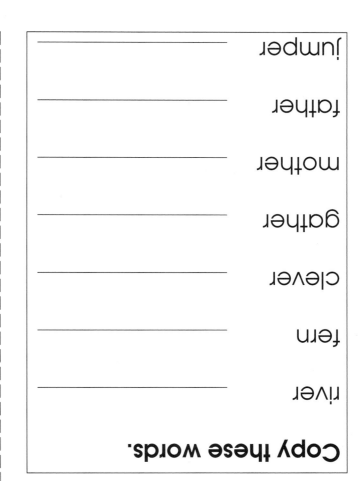

| f | | | |

| m | | | | | r |

| c | | | | |

er

fern

Draw pictures for these words.

bird

skirt

Copy these words.

first
_____

shirt
_____

bird
_____

third
_____

skirt
_____

thirst
_____

stir
_____

Find the 'ir' words.

F	I	R	S	T	J	G
T	R	R	D	I	C	I
H	S	K	I	R	T	R
I	T				H	L
R	I				I	R
D	R				R	B
E	C				S	I
K	S	V	I	R	T	R
B	L	H	S	C	F	D
S	H	I	R	T	A	G

ir

girl

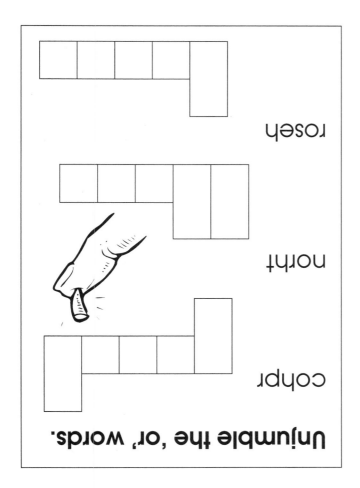

Unjumble the 'or' words.

cohpr

norht

roseh

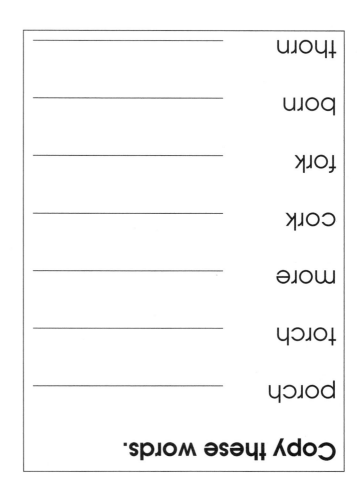

Copy these words.

porch _____

torch _____

more _____

cork _____

fork _____

born _____

thorn _____

Draw a fork and a torch on a horse.

or

horse

ur

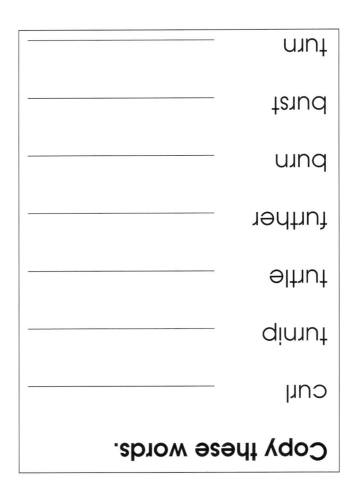

church

Copy these words.

curl

turnip

turtle

further

burn

burst

turn

Complete these 'ur' words.

t __ __ n

b __ __ st

b __ __ n

f __ __ th __ __

c __ __ l

t __ __ tle

Find and color the 'ur' words.

rsturnnbpturtlebds

hdcurlnhyuorsfurthermn

gchurchrtyburstbpunv

rsturnipmnburnmm

Match the 'ay' words to their meanings.

clay • • opposite of night

pay • • a type of earth

day • • dried grass

hay • • to give money for something

Copy these words.

play _____

hay _____

clay _____

bay _____

stay _____

day _____

pay _____

Circle the 'ay' words in the sentence. Draw a picture of the sentence.

'Children like to play in the hay.'

ay

bay

Match the 'ey' words to their pictures.

chimney

turkey

trolley

money

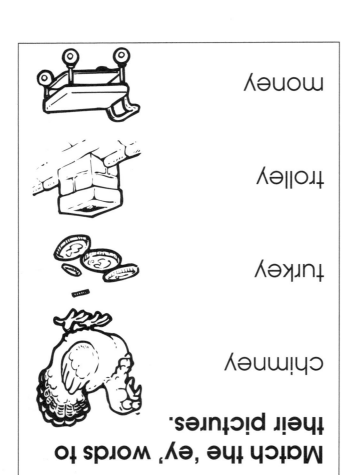

Copy these words.

jockey _____

turkey _____

donkey _____

money _____

chimney _____

key _____

trolley _____

Color the correct answer.

A jockey rides buses.
Yes   No

Smoke comes from a chimney.
Yes   No

A key is for opening locks.
Yes   No

A turkey is a bird.
Yes   No

ey

monkey

Copy these words.

shadow

narrow

hollow

slow

grow

know

row

Draw pictures for these words.

shadow

row

Find the 'ow' words.

S	H	A	D	O	W	N
L	K	C	O	O	C	A
O	N	B	A	W	R	R
W	O				O	R
K	W				W	O
B	C				E	W
C	D				O	K
O	W	G	R	O	W	L
R	O	W	A	O	W	K
H	O	L	L	O	W	R

OW

crow

Unjumble the 'oy' words.

yesrot

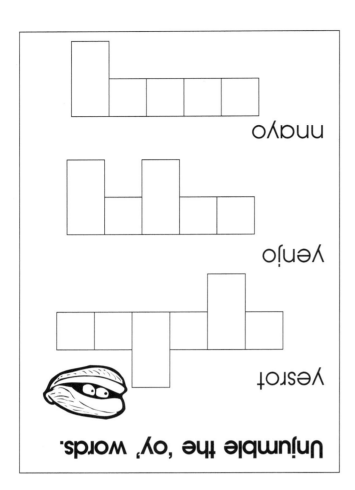

yenjo

nnayo

Copy these words.

joy

oyster

annoy

destroy

enjoy

toy

ahoy

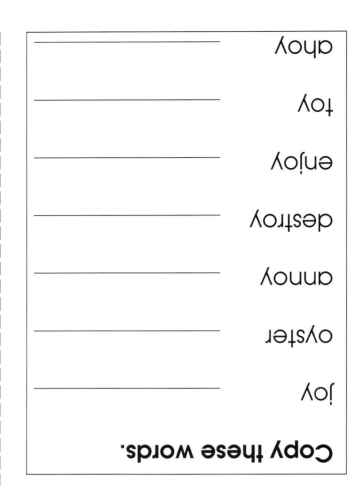

Draw a boy with a toy.

oy

boy

Draw pictures for these words.

plane

spade

Copy these words.

lake _____

grape _____

spade _____

plane _____

snake _____

game _____

cake _____

Find the 'a - e' words.

S	A	O	L	A	W	C
P	L	A	N	E	H	T
A	N	K	D	S	A	J
D	B				L	P
E	U				E	Q
K	E				M	C
E	R				L	A
G	A	M	E	V	A	K
H	E	S	N	A	K	E
I	G	R	A	P	E	A

a - e

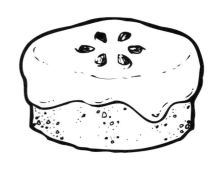

cake

Unjumble the 'ee' words.

eter

seeceh

tere

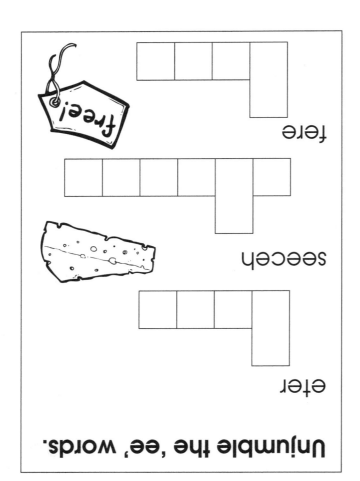

Copy these words.

sneeze _____

cheese _____

fifteen _____

cheep _____

free _____

see _____

freeze _____

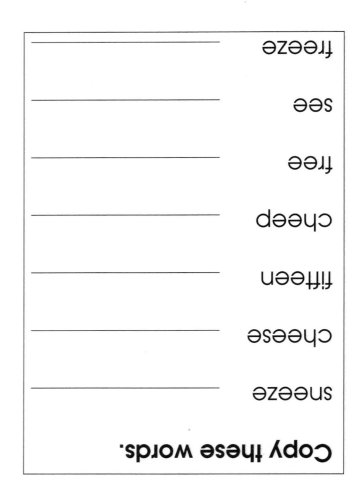

Draw a piece of cheese near a tree.

ee

tree

58   *Phonic Fold-Ups*   World Teachers Press

Complete these 'ie' words.

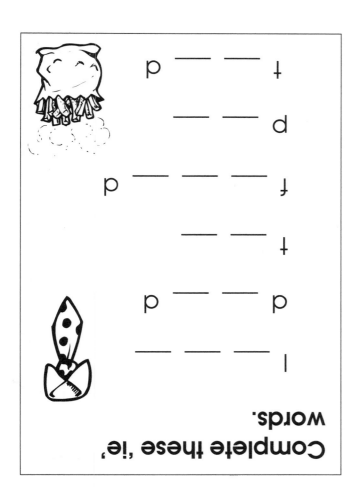

t __ __ p

p __ __

__ __ t

t __ __ p

p __ __ p

l __ __ __

Copy these words.

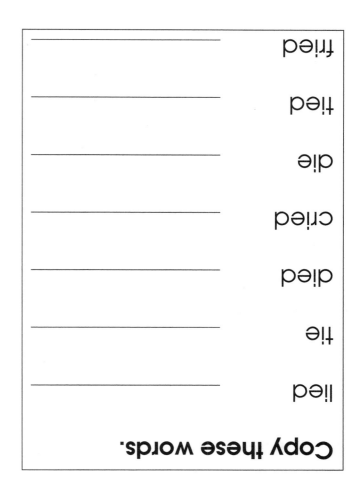

fried _____

tied _____

die _____

cried _____

died _____

tie _____

tied _____

Find and color the 'ie' words.

djsdtiedhgsfdtfriedmjhg
ldliednmeittiemgjh
lkmhdiednhdfcriednhik
sepienhfdfdiekhgs

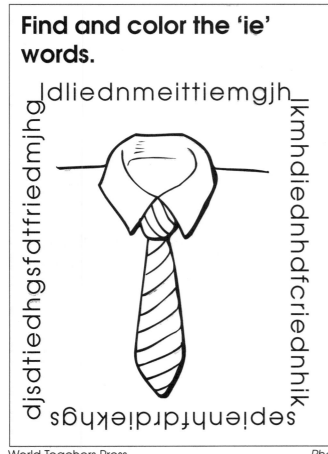

ie

cried

Match the 'i - e' words to their meanings.

- smile • • a place where bees live
- hive • • the skin of an animal
- pipe • • to widen the mouth
- hide • • a hollow tube

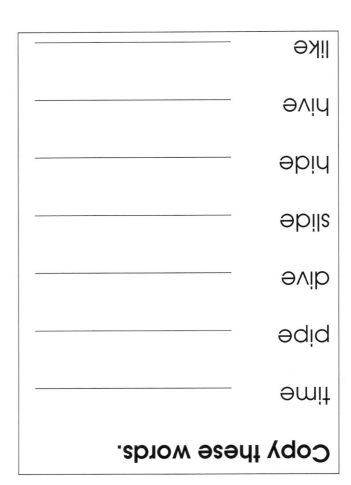

Copy these words.

time _____

pipe _____

dive _____

slide _____

hide _____

hive _____

like _____

Circle the 'i - e' words in the sentence. Draw a picture of the sentence.

'I like to hide in a pipe.'

i - e

diver

Match the 'o - e' words to their pictures.

stove

home

rope

stone

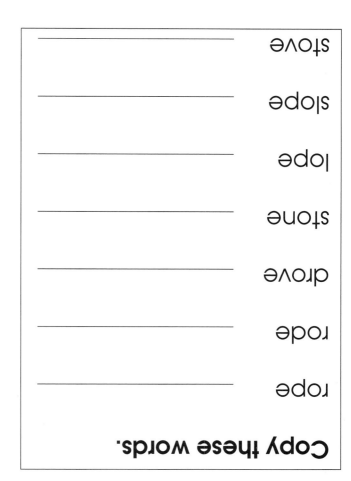

Copy these words.

rope

rode

drove

stone

lope

slope

stove

Color the correct answer.

A stove is used for cooking.
Yes   No

A rope is a type of snake.
Yes   No

A lope is a way of walking.
Yes   No

A stone is hard.
Yes   No

o - e

rode

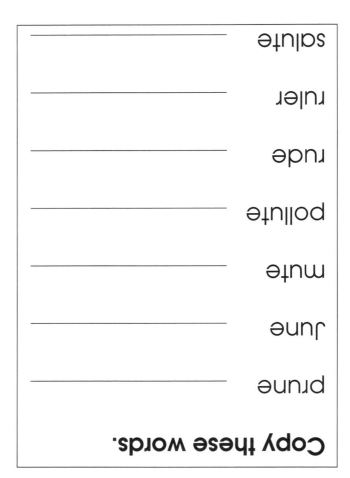

Copy these words.

prune

June

mute

pollute

rude

ruler

salute

Complete the 'u - e' words.

pr   r   poll

m   u - e   sal

Complete the crossword.

pollute
flute
salute
mute

u - e

flute

Draw pictures for these words.

goat

coach

Copy these words.

cloak _____

coast _____

coach _____

croak _____

goat _____

float _____

coat _____

Find the 'oa' words.

C	O	A	C	H	G	C
R	A	B	C	L	O	O
O	T	B	K	O	A	A
A	Y				T	S
K	I				C	T
N	S				L	E
A	M				O	P
F	L	O	A	T	A	O
C	O	A	T	O	K	U
B	I	R	B	O	A	T

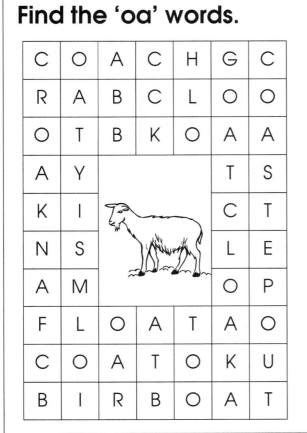

oa

boat

lipos

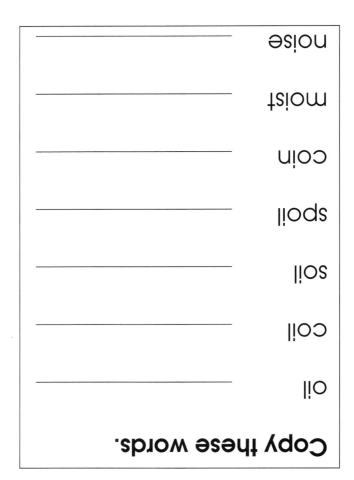

osnic

sitmo

Copy these words.

oil _____

coil _____

soil _____

spoil _____

coin _____

moist _____

noise _____

Draw a coin and some oil in the soil.

oi

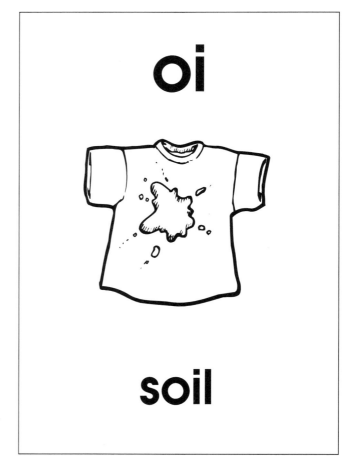

soil

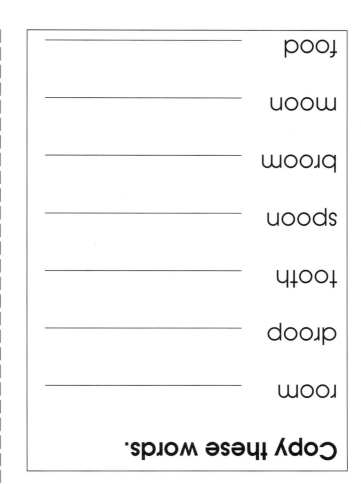

oo

boots

Complete these 'oo' words.

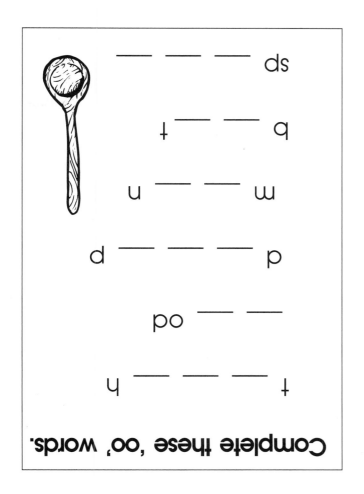

sp _ _ _

b _ _ t

m _ _ n

d _ _ _ _ p

_ _ _ oo

t _ _ _ _ h

Copy these words.

food _____

moon _____

broom _____

spoon _____

tooth _____

droop _____

room _____

Find and color the 'oo' words.

bonroomnbroomo
bpomoonhgomnffoodjh
pdroopnfosmtoothkgso
pmspoonmhbootgh

Copy these words.

cloud _____

house _____

found _____

loud _____

couch _____

round _____

sound _____

Match the 'ou' words to their meanings.

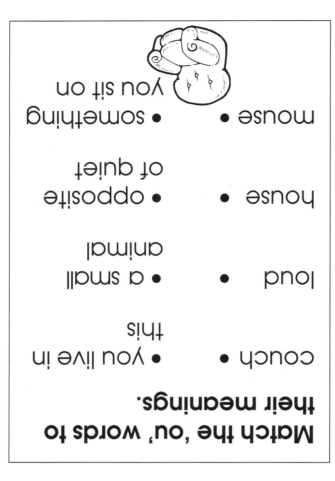

couch •   • you live in this

loud •   • a small animal

house •   • opposite of quiet

mouse •   • something you sit on

Circle the 'ou' words in the sentence. Draw a picture of the sentence.

'The mouse is sitting on the couch in the house.'

ou

mouse

Match the 'ai' words to their pictures.

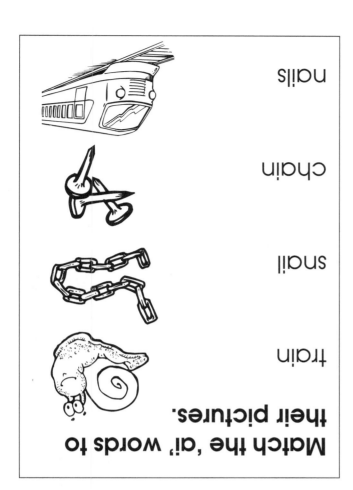

train

snail

chain

nails

Copy these words.

paint _____

mail _____

chain _____

nail _____

train _____

stain _____

sail _____

Color the correct answer.

A train is a type of car.
| Yes | No |

Rain comes from clouds.
| Yes | No |

A nail is used to hold wood together.
| Yes | No |

A stain is a type of boat.
| Yes | No |

ai

rain

meat

seat

speak

steam

clean

sea

peach

Copy these words.

Complete the crossword.

seat
steam
speak
meat
sea

s			

s	p		
	m		

ea

leaf

Draw pictures for these words.

chair

hair

Copy these words.

repair _____

dairy _____

chair _____

stair _____

pair _____

fairy _____

hair _____

Find the 'air' words.

D	F	A	F	A	I	R
A	A	E	B	C	A	E
I	I	S	A	K	R	P
R	R				I	A
Y	Y				R	I
Y	S				C	R
A	D				H	Y
H	A	I	R	B	A	I
C	E	F	P	A	I	R
S	T	A	I	R	R	P

air

fair

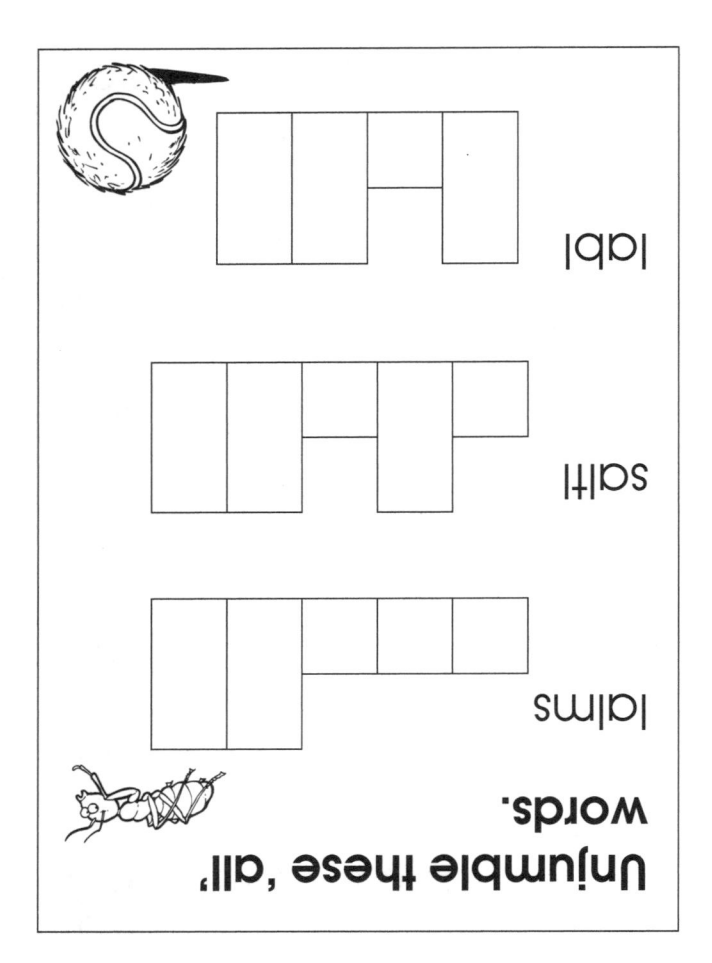

Unjumble these 'all' words.

labl

salti

lalms

Copy these words.

stall _____

fall _____

call _____

small _____

hall _____

recall _____

tall _____

Draw a tall girl with a small boy.

all

fall

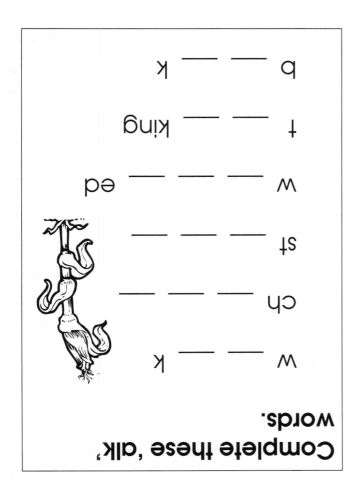

Complete these 'alk' words.

w — — — k

ch — — —

st — — —

w — — — ed

t — — — king

b — — k

Copy these words.

talk _____

walk _____

chalk _____

stalk _____

beanstalk _____

walked _____

talking _____

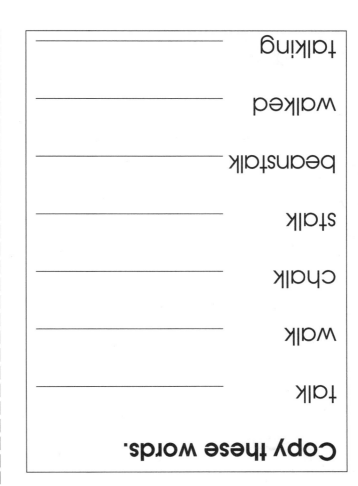

Find and color the 'alk' words.

beanstalknmstalkbgsteeswalkedmntalkingpnchalkfhkibalkmnbvzcvwalkinhhtalknbdat

---

alk

talk

---

ear

hear

Circle the 'ear' words in the sentence. Draw a picture of the sentence.

'I saw a tear appear from the child's eye."

Copy these words.

year ______

gear ______

tear ______

shear ______

fear ______

near ______

appear ______

Match the 'ear' words to their meanings.

appear • • comes from the eye

tear • • has 365 days

year • • scared

fear • • opposite of disappear

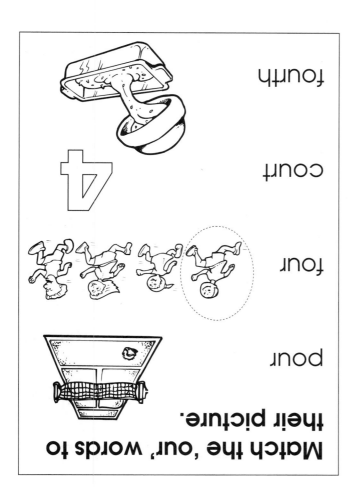

Match the 'our' words to their picture.

pour

four

court

fourth

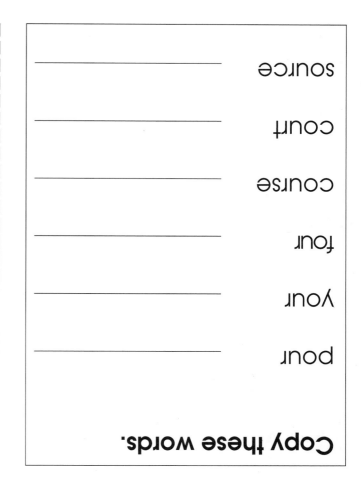

Copy these words.

pour _____

your _____

four _____

course _____

court _____

source _____

Color the correct answer.

Four is a number.

Yes   No

Course is a color.

Yes   No

You can pour water from a can.

Yes   No

Source is something that you put on food.

Yes   No

our

pour

Copy these words.

work

world

worst

worth

worn

world

worse

Complete the 'wor' words.

k

ld

th

wor

st

d

Complete the crossword.

world
worse
worst
word
worm

s | t

e

w

w | | | d

wor

world

Draw pictures for these words.

comb

thumb

Copy these words.

bomb ____________

thumb ____________

crumb ____________

limb ____________

numb ____________

comb ____________

climb ____________

Find the 'mb' words.

T	H	U	M	B	B	B
A	G	P	B	T	F	O
C	R	U	M	B	O	M
L	E				O	B
I	R				D	L
M	A				J	A
B	K				U	M
H	S	M	L	I	M	B
B	L	I	C	O	M	B
N	U	M	B	M	C	N

mb

lamb

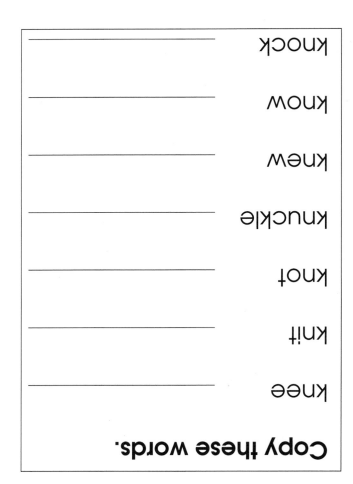

Copy these words.

knee _____

knit _____

knot _____

knuckle _____

knew _____

know _____

knock _____

Unjumble the 'kn' words.

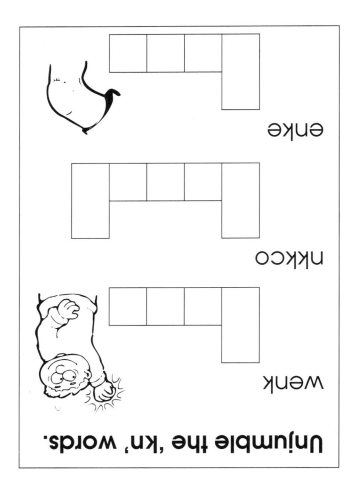

wenk

nkkco

enke

Draw a knife in a knot of a tree.

kn

knife

Phonic Fold-Ups

Complete each 'a' words.

b _ _ ket

g _ _ _ s

f _ th _

c _ _ le

p _ t

p _ h

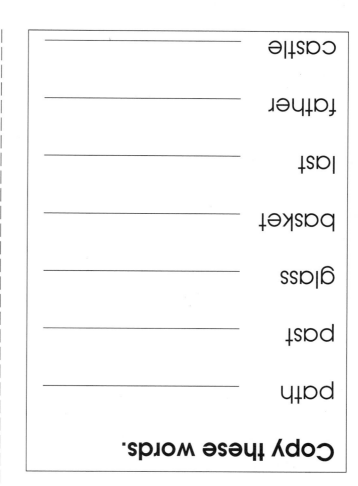

Copy these words.

castle _____

father _____

last _____

basket _____

glass _____

past _____

bath _____

Find and color the 'a' words.

mnbacastlehglassl
sdbasketnhdapathwnal
bshbathfgdfatherhgad
sapasthndlastimng

a

bath

Copy these words.

dove _____

shovel _____

nothing _____

monkey _____

Monday _____

money _____

sponge _____

Match the 'o' words to their meanings.

glove • • a garden tool

shovel • • an animal

monkey • • worn on the hand

dove • • needed to buy things

money • • a bird

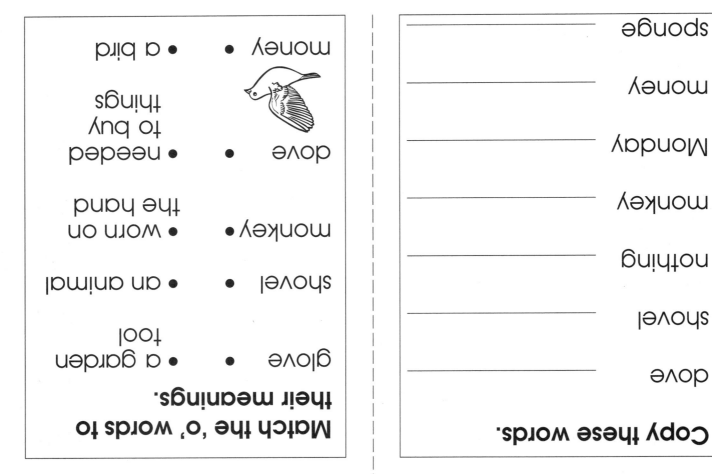

Circle the 'o' words in the sentence. Draw a picture of the sentence.

'The monkey has a lot of money.'

O

glove

Match the 'o' words to their pictures.

clover

tomato

potato

post

Copy these words.

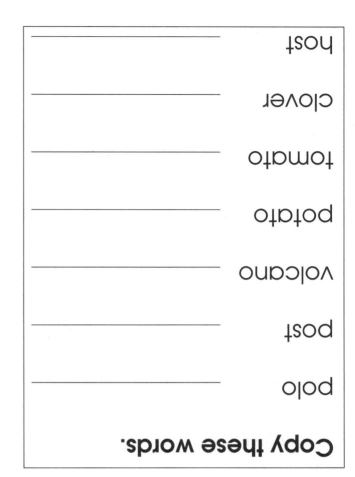

host _____

clover _____

tomato _____

potato _____

volcano _____

post _____

polo _____

Color the correct answer.

Clover is a plant.
| Yes | | No |

A potato is a type of vegetable.
| Yes | | No |

A volcano is a very large river.
| Yes | | No |

A tomato is a fruit.
| Yes | | No |

O

clover

Copy these words.

rifle

puddle

needle

little

poodle

eagle

jungle

Complete the 'le' words.

need   rit   pudd

egg   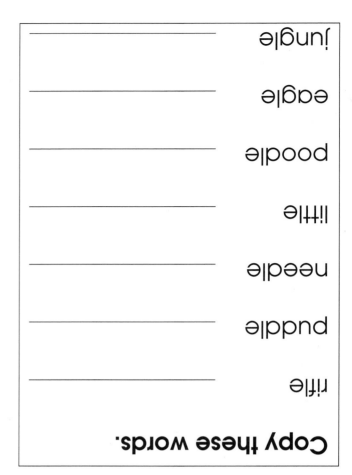 le   jung

---

Complete the crossword.

poodle   puddle

little   beetle

---

le

poodle

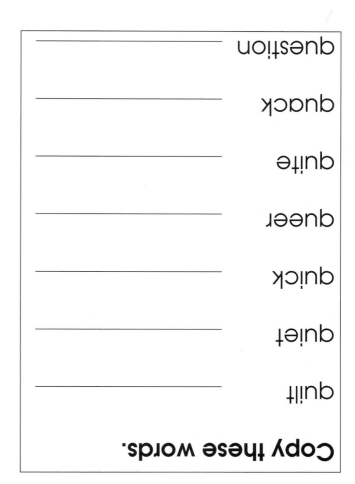

Complete these 'qu' words.

qu __ e

qu __ t

qu __ r

qu __ u

qu __ t

qu __ k

Copy these words.

quilt _____

quiet _____

quick _____

queer _____

quite _____

quack _____

question _____

Find and color the 'qu' words.

saquiltnnqusqueernqum
wquestionnbquick
psqueenkganquacknbd
lquietnfqvquitemn

---

qu

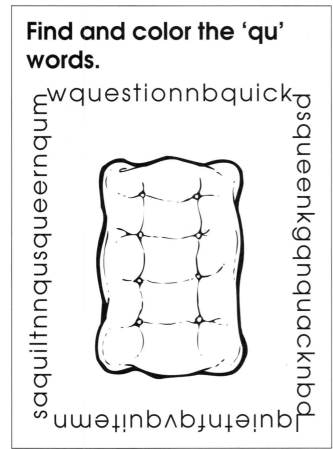

queen

Match the 'wa' words to their meanings.

wallet • • an insect

water • • used to hold money

waddle • • You drink this

wasp • • a type of walk

Copy these words.

water _____

wallet _____

wander _____

wash _____

waddle _____

walk _____

wasp _____

Circle the 'wa' words in the sentence. Draw a picture of the sentence.

'The wasp had a wash in the water.'

wa

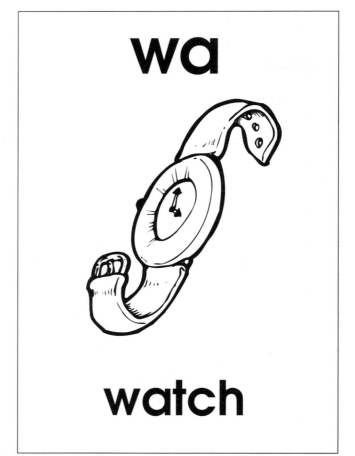

watch

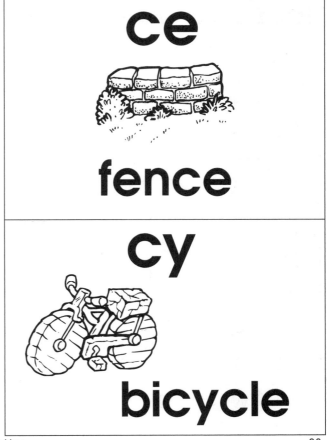

Copy these words.

sentence

palace

celery

prince

cellar

cymbal

fence

Complete the 'ce' and 'cy' words.

ten   ce   prin

mbal   cy   bi

Complete the crossword.

sentence
prince
fence
celery

ce

fence

cy

bicycle

Copy these words.

race

place

disgrace

spice

nice

twice

rice

Draw pictures for these words.

race

spice

Find the 'ice' and 'ace' words.

R	I	C	E	J	R	D
F	N	I	C	E	A	I
A	C	C	A	C	C	S
C	G				E	G
E	D				P	R
C	I				R	A
D	C				F	C
I	E	P	L	A	C	E
E	S	P	I	C	E	F
T	W	I	C	E	G	H

NUTME

ice

dice

ace

face

Unjumble the 'ge' and 'gi' words.

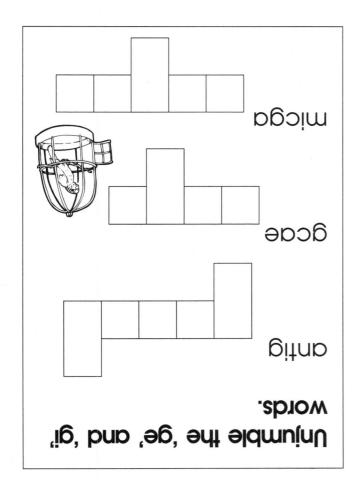

micga

gcae

antig

Copy these words.

rage _____

page _____

cabbage _____

stage _____

magic _____

engine _____

giant _____

Draw a giant with a magic cage.

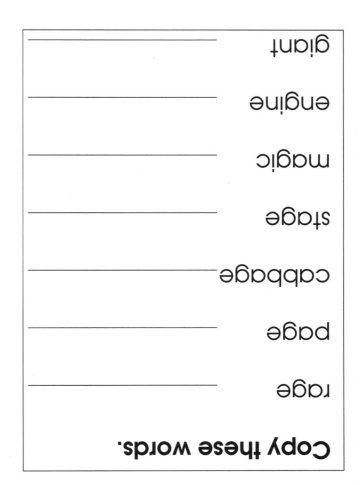

ge

page

gi

magic